MW01289513

THE FORCE AND LAW OF GIVING AND RECEIVING

Copyright (C) by: Paul Olashore2018

Published by Revelation Books Ventures.

paulolashore@yahoo.com

+2348099009020

1

TABLE OF CONTENTS

CHAPTER ONE

LAW OF GIVING AND RECEIVING

John 3:16

"For God so loved the world, that he gave his only begotten Son, that whosoever believeth in him should not perish, but have everlasting life."

Luke 6:38

"Give, and it shall be given unto you; good measure, pressed down, and shaken together, and running over, shall men give into your bosom. For with the same measure that ye mete withal it shall be measured to you again."

Gen 22:15 — 18

"And the angel of the Lord called unto Abraham out of heaven the second time, And said, By myself have I sworn, saith the Lord, for because thou hast done this thing, and hast not withheld thy son, thine only son: That in blessing I will bless thee, and in multiplying I will multiply thy seed as the stars of the heaven, and as the sand which is upon the sea shore; and thy seed shall possess the gate of his enemies; And in thy seed shall all the nations of the earth be blessed; because thou hast obeyed my voice."

The whole realms of existence are run by laws, forces and systems that God has set there to help us live and enjoy all that is available in them all. Some laws operate only in the physical while others operate only in the spiritual. Quantum physics studies are showing us now that the laws in the quantum dimension are different from the laws the scientists use in the normal physical level. However, there are some laws that are universal and work in all realms and levels of existence.

These universal laws are the same in all realms. They are a constant in all realms. These laws are above all other laws. Paul said against such (these laws) there is no law. They cannot be limited by the structure and functionality of any realm. They are able to manifest and obtain results in all realms. These laws are all expressions of God's Nature. One of them is **Love**. Another is **Giving**. They all birth fruits in all realms. Whether it is the physical realm, the spiritual realm or the thought realm, they are able to bear fruit in all realms.

Now it is good to know that behind every law is a force. The force is what makes the law to work and be consistent. The force of gravity for example supports the law of gravity. The law only operates where the force is. The law is non-existent without the force. It is the introduction of the force that brings the law into manifestation. Create a force and you will be establishing a law.

One of the most important forces to understand is the Force of Giving and Receiving. A Universal force runs the Law of Giving and Receiving. God has wired this entire universe to run on this law. Whatever you give within this universe both in the spirit and in the physical comes back to you in multiplied form. If we give trouble, we receive a lot of the same. If we give good, we also reap a lot of it too. Give gratitude and you reap more favour. Give a smile and reap many smiles.

Give hope and you will reap encouragement. Give love and you will reap plenty of love. Bless and you will reap more blessing. Give forgiveness an you will reap forgiveness from God and men. Give good attitude, motive, and you will reap a lot of good attitude and motive from people that would come around you. The energy you send out to the universe is what God has commanded that you will reap.

Jesus by whom and through whom all things are made, who also is the sustaining force and substance of the whole realms of existence made a profound statement about this when he said, *"Give and it shall be given to you, good measure, pressed down, shaken together and running over"*. He was simply telling us about a law that they (the Holy Trinity) have put in place in the universe that does not fail.

There is a need for you as a child of God, (Child of the Creator of the Universe) to develop skill in operating this law in your favour and in the favour of the kingdom of God that you are a part of.

God set up this universe to run on

laws and forces. The laws keep all things in both the spiritual and physical realm the way He wants it. The laws are kept in operation by the forces behind the laws. The Force of Giving and Receiving is the Force that sets up a harvest after the Giving part of the Law is activated. This same thing happens when the Force of Gravity, which operates the law of Gravity, makes all things that go up on earth to come down.

The force of giving and receiving makes the law of giving and receiving effective. It sets the process of harvest even when we cannot see it and guarantees the delivery of harvest for every true giving. Every giving must have a receiving and every true giving must definitely have a proper receiving. It is a law that works all over the universe and those who have mastered how to engage it in their favour rule the universe.

Forces bring in the energy needed into an environment to create and make happen what they are set to make happen. The Force of Gravity brings the energy necessary to draw everyone and all things on earth to the center of the earth, which is what keeps us all here otherwise we would all be floating endlessly in space.

Giving is a universal law that multiplies all things in all realms of existence. When we give, we activate the multiplication of what we have given and other extra things added.

CHAPTER TWO

GIVING FROM THE HEART

Giving starts from the heart. The heart has to truly give something before we can have multiplication set in motion. When God asked Abraham to give Isaac, He did not need Abraham to kill Isaac for it to be recorded that he had given him. As soon as he did it in his heart and took the knife to kill his son, it was counted to have been done. Your heart has to give something before your hands release it. It is at the point when your heart gives something that it's counted or recorded as given. At that point, the Law of harvest kicks off. This is why sometimes we find ourselves experiencing the harvest coming in even before we have given the money or help. This happens because as soon as you decide to give something towards the advancement of God's Kingdom for example. The moment a decision comes from your heart, it is counted as done just as it was counted for Abraham relevant to giving his son to God. God does not take human sacrifice. But Abraham did not know this, the Bible said he believe that after he must have killed his son Isaac, God is able to raise him from the dead. *Hebrews 11:17-19*

Giving has to come from the heart. Our hearts must decide to be obedient to the giving of our tithes, kingdom seeds, offerings, prophet's seed, seed to parents and seed to the needy. As soon as obeying these different types of seeding is coming from a heart, which has decided to fully obey God, giving becomes easy. We only find grace for what our hearts are made up to observe. Our giving is not only consistent when it is coming from our hearts, but it continues to be consistent even when harvest is delayed because our hearts see honouring and being obedient to God more important than having the harvest. This is what Paul meant when he said that Jesus said, *"it is more blessed to give them to receive"* Acts *20:35*. The heart that is more focused on the obedience of giving is more blessed than the one focussed on receiving.

CHAPTER THREE

GIVING OUT OF LOVE AND OBEDIENCE

Giving works in all realms. If you give in the spirit, you will reap a harvest. If you give in the physical, you will reap a harvest. God is a Giver and therefore giving is one His Attributes. Giving and Receiving is therefore a law and it works in all realms. God owns all things and therefore His Nature works in all realms.

Whatever thing or experience you want to multiply, once you give it, you have just activated the harvest or multiplication process that will bring multiples of that experience to you. It is so simple. Give it and you have just multiplied it. Only make sure you are

giving it from your heart with the
motive of Love and Obedience. Giving
and Receiving is a law to which all
realms in the Universe respond
positively.

Give a job and you will reap many
jobs. The kind of jobs you need. Give a
smile, and you will reap many smiles
even in places where they do not
smile at all. Give money and you will
reap money. Give help and you will
get many help where you need it most
and in other areas of your life.
Now, the Lord wants you to give in
love and obedience when you give.
Give with love for giving or for the

person or thing receiving your gift. Give out of love for people that need you giving. Be genuine about it. Give out love also for the advancement of God's Kingdom on earth. It makes your giving to count in the spiritual courts of reward. Give also because you love giving as your Father in Heaven who is a Giver too. God loves giving and gives to people because He loves them. God loves a cheerful giver. Give because you want to be a Giver like your Heavenly Father. He is a Giver and at the core of His Nature is Love, which is characterised by giving. Therefore seek to be a Giver like your father and you will find super abundant grace in giving and growing in the same. God actually commands us to give in all the different areas I mentioned earlier because He wants to see that His Nature is fully manifested in us all.

Give in obedience. Give because God commanded it. Our obedience to God attracts unusual and great rewards from Him. Our obedience is proof that His Nature is maturing in us. God counts obedience and it is always rated highly in His Presence. Cornelius' obedience in giving to support the poor was rated highly in God's Presence that Heaven had to arrange a carrier of the gospel to reach him. And no surprise that his whole household got saved and baptized in the Holy Ghost all at once by the Power of the Holy Ghost. See the reward of good works of giving to the poor.

Once we give from our hearts in love and obedience, and these conditions are met in giving, you are guaranteed a harvest of what you give and more.

Give your tithes in obedience to God's command, not in fear of His Judgment and you will see the promised harvest of blessings, protection, expansion and peace. Give it also with love for God's Kingdom. Give it with passion to make sure God's Kingdom does not lack. Give to support every unique assignment of the part of the body of Christ to which you belong. Give consistently towards this in obedience to *Psalms 68:13* and out of love for the progress of His Purposes on earth and He will make you great and mighty on the earth. Give to support and honour your parents whether they are in need or not. The Bible called this action the first commandment with blessings attached. *Ephesians 6:2*-3. The blessing is that it will be well with you. You will always have all you need financially, emotionally, physically and every way. The second blessing is that you will have the grace of long life. Death will be distant to you.

Give to your spiritual parents. Your Pastors are your spiritual parents who are also the Prophets that God has set over your life. This also includes every visiting Man of God that blesses you on your Church's platform. The Bible says you should give to all who teach you. *Galatians 6:*6. Give to your Pastor (Prophet) because it invokes a greater dimension of God's blessings on your life. You also receive the Prophet's reward of seeing His Words come to pass speedily in your life. Amazing things take place when you do this consistently, either monthly or bimonthly. Be wise and do it out of obedience to God's Word and out of love for God and your pastor.

Give to help the needy. The poor around you must have something from what God blesses you with. Make it a habit to always look for someone that is poor to bless from time to time. You can do it anonymously if you feel you might come under pressure from those people. However, give out of obedience to God and compassion for the people you are helping. Give from your heart. In addition, be sensitive to the needs of those you consider not poor, but that you can help. Someone might not be poor but could be in need of a drink and might not be able to buy because he forgot his wallet at home. Offer to buy them a drink. You have helped someone in need. Jesus said, *"as much as you have done it for the least of my brothers* (New Creation People), *you have done it for me"*. Be cheerful in whatever is in your capacity to give to either rich or poor. *Galatians 6:9-10*

Give, give, give. It is the love and obedience way.

CHAPTER FOUR

GIVE WITH EXPECTATION TO RECEIVE

29

Give with expectation of the harvest. Give no room to thoughts that there is no harvest to giving otherwise you will be setting in motion energies that will resist your due harvest. This is simply Satan setting you up to resist your harvest by using your own powers against you.

Give whatever you can to support the less privileged or the poor and you would have helped someone. This activates a lot of help for you. Just make sure your motive is as obedience to God or for love or both. Harvest is activated that moment. However, expect harvest. Your expectation is

important and God has commanded
what your expectation should be.
Simply obey that. Do not just have the
right giving attitude, motive and heart.
Make sure you have the right position
of heart also for receiving the harvest
that God has promised for every
giving. It is about the integrity of God
keeping His Promises to you.

If you are not expecting a harvest,
then your spiritual antenna will not be
reaching out to receive and Satan can
take advantage of this to create delay
of all the blessing you have activated
through your giving. God has
commanded all realms to deliver
harvest towards every right giving. So

expect your harvest and have faith
that it has come.

CHAPTER FIVE

WE REAP WHAT WE GIVE

Luke 6:38

"Give, and it shall be given unto you; good measure, pressed down, and shaken together, and running over, shall men give into your bosom. For with the same measure that ye mete withal it shall be measured to you again."

When we give, what we give we reap. If you give a job, you will reap many jobs that you need. When you give help, you will get a lot of help. When you give money, you will get a lot of it. When you give open doors, you will reap a lot too. What you give you reap. However, many times, you get more than what you reap. Abraham got multiplication of children. God gave him more through Israel the nation and the the multitude of born again people that have lived and will live. *Galatians 3:29*

Apart from the physical children, Abraham got more blessing. God said he is getting more blessing because he did not withhold his son from him. God multiplied his blessings and multiplied what He had given him even before this test. Whatever, you give; God will multiply and give you extra for other areas of your life.

Therefore, we have to be careful what we give everyday. It will come back to us in a harvest. If you sow discord among people, you will reap discord. If you backbite and slander people to destroy their image, you will have it back in multiply measures. It is therefore important that we are careful about how we live our lives. The command to live like Christ is not just for us to please our Father in Heaven. It is also to help reduce and escape reaping many bad experiences in life. Conforming to Christ saves us from much danger and positions us for the best things and experiences in life.

Whatever you sow, you will reap.

A bicycle knocked down a man and his son was informed. The son however, never went to check his father until the old man died. He too was knocked down by a motorcycle and his son refused to go check on him too until he died. He sowed a wrong seed to his parent. He did not show care and therefore he could not reap care. I still wonder what would happen to his son.

We must be careful how we treat people, because soon we would receive the same treatment in many

measures. Dr Mike Murdock said,
"What you make happen for others,
God (through the law of giving and
receiving) will make happen for you.

Therefore, if you have sowed negative
seeds and you want to escape. You
need to go God in genuine repentance
and get forgiveness. Then God will do
what He does. He will root out all
plants He has not planted in you and
great things will start happening.

Giving brings to us harvest like the one
we have never known. Be faithful.

CHAPTER SIX

PRAYER POINTS

PRAYER FOR SALVATION

Pray the following prayer to experience the new birth and become a child of God.

Father, I do not want to be a sinner anymore. Please forgive me my sins. I believe that Jesus Christ died for my sins and was raised from the dead for my salvation. I accept and confess Jesus as my Lord and Saviour. Jesus, come into me, live in me and through me In Jesus Name, Amen.

If you said this prayer sincerely from your heart, you are born again. Write me on

pstpaul@elohimstabernacle.org.
Please read two chapters of the bible every day starting from Matthew. Pray every morning and evening. If you are in Lagos, Nigeria, join me every Sunday at Elohim's Tabernacle. If you are not in Lagos, join our live streaming every Sunday.

For venue, service and streaming details, log on to www.elohimstabernacle.org.

PRAYERS TO ACTIVATE THE LAW OF GIVING AND RECEIVING

- Father, I receive the grace you have made available to be a Giver like You in Jesus Mighty Name.

- Father, help me to understand clearly the principle of giving in Jesus Mighty Name.

- Father, I receive grace to give from my heart always in Jesus Mighty Name.

- Father, give me a clear revelation of the law of giving and receiving in Jesus Mighty Name.

- Father, help me always have the right motive for giving. Fill my heart with love for giving as You want me to and willingness to obey You in giving in Jesus Mighty Name.

- Father, help me never miss any opportunity to give. Please make me a Giver like You in Jesus Mighty Name
(C)2018 Paul Olashore

Made in the USA
Coppell, TX
26 July 2022